Original title:
Fruit of the Season

Copyright © 2025 Creative Arts Management OÜ
All rights reserved.

Author: Benjamin Caldwell
ISBN HARDBACK: 978-1-80586-469-1
ISBN PAPERBACK: 978-1-80586-941-2

Harvest Moon Magic

Under the moon, the pumpkins grin,
Squirrels dance, let the fun begin!
Apples bob in a merry race,
While all the pears try to outpace.

Ciders bubbling, oh what a sight,
A fruit parade, it's pure delight!
Peaches plot their sticky schemes,
As grapes burst forth with fizzy dreams.

Splendor of the Fields

Corn cobs are wearing hats, so neat,
Carrots strut on their leafy feet.
Beets blush red; they just can't hide,
While radishes roll with comical pride.

Scarecrows chuckle at the scene,
As cabbages join in, looking keen.
Sunflowers wave their tall, green arms,
Saying, 'Join us, we bring the charms!'

Rhythms of Harvest

The rhythm of the crunching apples,
Makes even rabbits do funny chapels.
Cherries giggle when they drop,
While melons bounce, they just can't stop.

Oranges are jiving in a zesty line,
Lemons laugh, 'We're sour but fine!'
Ripe bananas peel back with glee,
'Come dance with us, oh can't you see?'

Prismatic Pleasures

Berries burst in a rainbow spree,
While lemons play hide-and-seek with trees.
Jellybeans tumble, oh what a sight,
As grapes go rolling, full of delight.

Lychees giggle, all soft and sweet,
Mangoes swing to their juicy beat.
Kiwis wear sunglasses, looking quite cool,
While figs strut around, feeling like fools!

Ripening Echoes

In the tree, a banana sings,
Swinging low, it teeters and swings.
A pear, in laughter, rolls away,
Saying, 'Catch me if you may!'

A bunch of grapes starts a race,
Wobbling fast, what a funny chase!
They trip on vines, a comical scene,
With giggles echoing, crisp and clean.

The Golden Harvest

A pumpkin struts in a patch of sun,
Wearing a smile, it thinks it's fun.
Carrots cheer with leafy toes,
Dancing wildly, striking poses.

Maize wears glasses, big and round,
Claiming it's the best in town.
With every wiggle, a pop and a crack,
It jazzes up the garden track.

A Symphony of Flavors

Cherries are drumming on pots and pans,
While lemons dance with olive fans.
A melon juggles seeds with glee,
Yelling, 'Look at me, look at me!'

Peaches pirouette, a joyous pair,
With nectarines flipping through the air.
Their fruity tunes burst out in style,
A sweetened concert that makes you smile.

The Orchard's Lullaby

In the orchard, an apple snorring,
Dreaming of pies and folks adoring.
A fig on a branch plays a tune,
Swaying gently 'neath the moon.

A berry brigade joins in for fun,
Singing songs till the day is done.
They giggle and tumble, a cozy nest,
In this merry land, they know they're blessed.

Sweet Simplicity

In the orchard, apples grin,
Waving leaves, where do we begin?
Peaches blush like shy old friends,
Their juicy gossip never ends.

Berries scatter like confetti bright,
Inviting bees to join the flight.
Lemons laughing, zesty and bold,
They chat with limes, tales to unfold.

Seasons of Abundance

Orange pumpkins stack like chairs,
Waiting for a feast of stares.
Pineapples wear their crowns so proud,
While grapes are dancing in a crowd.

Bananas slip with silly grace,
Chasing mangoes in a race.
Fruits unite, a comical crew,
In a kitchen's lively hue.

Nature's Palette

Raspberry red on a sunlit vine,
Cherries giggle over sweetened wine.
Kiwi whispers secrets untold,
As green starts to sparkle like gold.

Watermelons splash in summer's glow,
Filling faces with laughter and flow.
Pears in pairs, they schmooze and sway,
Declaring themselves the stars of the day.

Marmalade Dreams

Jars lined up like soldiers neat,
Each one bursting with a treat.
Funky figs and luscious rhyme,
Spread the joy; it's marmalade time!

Strawberries float like boats on a jam,
A toast to the morning, with claps and a slam.
Grapefruit wakes with a zesty cheer,
Stirring laughter along with the beer.

Fruits of Time

In the orchard, apples swing,
They wear their coats, blushing pink.
Bananas dance, in pairs they cling,
While pears and plums share a wink.

Cherries chatter, round they roll,
Grapes gossip on the vine.
Melon joins, it's on a stroll,
A picnic plot, just so fine!

Dances in the Orchard

Peaches twirl in summer's glow,
Limes limbo low, tightrope show.
Figs flip-flop, so light and spry,
As oranges bounce and lemons fly.

With every leap, they giggle loud,
A fruity parade, a circus proud.
Coconuts join with a big ol' thud,
The orchard shakes with laughter and mud!

Taste of the Solstice

Raspberries wear tiny hats of cream,
Watermelons burst and giggle, it seems.
Blueberries dance on a cupcake spree,
While lemons squirt jokes, just to be free.

Strawberries sing with a sweet little song,
Tart cherries chime in, playing along.
The sun shines bright, the laughter flows,
In this (mostly) quiet, fruity hall of prose.

Savoring the Season

Mangoes hoot, with zest they clink,
Kiwi hops on, let's all rethink.
Pineapples prance like they own the show,
And berries invited, just to glow.

Each fruit finds a partner, with giggles and spins,
Crafting a jamboree, where everyone wins.
They prattle and play until stars start to peep,
In the orchard of joy, where none will sleep!

The Taste of Time

In spring, the cherries wear a grin,
While apples plot their cheeky spin.
Bananas dance with yellow glee,
As oranges giggle, "Look at me!"

Berry bushes play hide and seek,
While peaches blush, feeling unique.
Grapes in their clusters, all in a frame,
Say, "Let's get together, we're all the same!"

Melons roll and claim their throne,
In this patch, they're never alone.
They whisper secrets to the sun,
Laughing together, always fun!

And when autumn's tendrils weave,
The pears chuckle, "You won't believe!"
With laughter ringing through the trees,
They boast of wisdom, if you please!

Orchard's Lullaby

In a grove where apples sway,
Lemons joke, "It's a bright new day!"
Mangoes serenade the breeze,
While bananas strut with swagger, ease.

Cherries chuckle, "We're so sweet,"
As they roll out with sprightly feet.
Grapefruits puff and say, "We're fine,
Join us for a zesty time!"

Pears whisper tales, all juicy, bright,
Of summertime and pure delight.
Peaches twirl like dancers bold,
While wild strawberries claim the gold.

Through laughter's echo, joy takes flight,
In this orchard's charm, hearts feel light.
A funky rhythm, nature's melody,
In every bite, pure symphony!

Sweetened Interlude

A pineapple wears a crown so grand,
While berries form a silly band.
With laughter bursting all around,
They dance upon the vibrant ground.

Watermelons in a rolling spree,
Say, "Who's got the best Jolly Glee?"
Limes chime in, "Let's all unite,
In truth, we're zesty, quite the sight!"

Bananas slip with playful tricks,
While nuts and figs perfect their mix.
They toast to the vines, all suave and sleek,
In every taste, a cheeky peek!

With every crunch, a joke unfolds,
As the ripeness of laughter surely molds.
In this sweetened, fruity parade,
A giggle here, a snack well-made!

Ripened Reflections

As morning dew meets plum's soft cheek,
A raspberry claims the spotlight, sleek.
The oranges chuckle, full and round,
While tangerines roll, without a sound.

Grapes start gossip with a wink,
Sipping juice, they never sink.
Peanuts tag along, oh what a crew,
In this fruity world, there's always a view!

Fig leaves wave like tender hands,
While ripened fruits make merry plans.
They nod to the breeze, "Let's have some fun,
It's a fruity thrill like no other run!"

As daylight fades, the stand-up show,
Berries giggle, "We steal the glow!"
In this harvest of joy, take a seat,
For laughter and sweetness, we can't be beat!

Harvested Whispers

In the orchard, apples chat,
Telling tales of a pie so flat.
Pears can't help but roll with glee,
As cherries giggle, "Look at me!"

Squirrels snack on the nuts they find,
While grapes pop jokes, oh so unkind.
"Why did the banana go to school?"
"To get a-peeling, that's the rule!"

Peaches tease, in fuzzy pride,
As lemons pucker, lips collide.
Melons join with a silly grin,
Singing, "Let the harvest begin!"

When night falls, stars start to gleam,
Fruits dream sweetly, as in a dream.
With laughter echoing through the night,
The orchard's tales are pure delight.

Nectar's Kiss

Buzzing bees start planning traps,
For a taste of nectar, oh the mishaps!
"Here's my plan," the orange said,
"Let's make juice till we're all red!"

Lemons laugh, all bitter and bright,
"Make lemonade, stir up some fright!"
Bananas slip, in comedic flair,
Landing straight on a hyena's hair!

Figs flaunt their soft plump skin,
As berries battle, who will win?
The grapes just hang, swaying with ease,
"Let's all dance!" and they giggle with tease.

The sun dips low, casting a glow,
Nature's laughter puts on a show.
With a kiss of nectar, sweet and fun,
The orchard parties till day is done.

Orchard Dreams

In dreams of apples, cider flows,
While dancing figs wear fancy clothes.
Cherries waltz and do a spin,
While peaches burst with a cheeky grin.

Grapes gather round, they tell a joke,
"Why did the orange stop and poke?
Because it saw a juicy prank,
And decided to roll down the plank!"

Pineapples wear crowns made of green,
As lemons sip tea, feeling so keen.
Plums toss jokes, ripe and round,
While strawberries giggle, "What a sound!"

As night whispers secrets, fruity and light,
The orchard chuckles beneath the starlight.
In this land where laughter's the theme,
Fruits blossom bright in a whimsical dream.

Bounty's Embrace

In a patch of pumpkins, 'tis a sight,
They shout, "We glow with all our might!"
Cucumbers chuckle, wiggling around,
While zucchini jokes just astound.

The apples think they're the best in town,
But pears wear crowns and walk with a frown.
"Let's make cider!" they all proclaim,
While berries argue over the name!

Tomatoes blushing with a fiery hue,
Whispering secrets just to a few.
"Why did the lemon start to play?
To zest up the party in a grand way!"

Under the stars, they join in cheer,
Fruits and veggies, all gather near.
In this bounty, laughter does lace,
A deliciously silly, joyous embrace.

Crispy Creations

In the crunchy land of pear,
Where apples play tag without care,
Lemons laugh with zestful glee,
While bananas dance by the tree.

Cabbage tries to steal the show,
But the grapes just giggle, "Oh no!"
Radishes blush, thinking they're sweet,
As cherries roll out on tiny feet.

A stubborn nut wants to claim fame,
But avocados just tease, what a game!
Kiwi juggles his fuzzy allure,
While the bouncy berries yell, "We're pure!"

Peaches pout, feeling quite ripe,
Oranges boast, "We're the type!"
When the harvest moon starts to rise,
All partake in nature's surprise!

Tales from the Orchard

Once in an orchard full of cheer,
The plums held a party, it was clear,
Peaches wore hats made of leaves,
While cherries played pranks, oh how they tease!

One day a pumpkin tried to roll,
But got stuck in the grass, oh poor soul!
Carrots came over, laughing with glee,
Said, "Stay still, we'll pour you some tea!"

An apple brought in jokes from a book,
And every single pear had to look,
The beets made faces, looking so red,
While the cucumbers danced on their heads!

In the corner, a melon played tunes,
Drawing in critters, the kids and raccoons,
When dusk would bring shadows from trees,
The orchard would giggle, such fun never flees!

The Lush Retreat

In a garden that seemed quite absurd,
Lettuce fibbed, saying, "I never heard!"
Tomatoes blushed, they shaped their fears,
As radishes chuckled, stopped up their tears.

A pear held a disco, with music so loud,
While the squashes formed a shimmying crowd,
The herbs got together, forming a band,
Basil hit snare, cilantro waved his hand.

User berries laughed till they cried,
"Is that an eggplant who just tried to glide?"
The pumpkins were rolling, all out of sync,
As beets wore their coats, all pink, in a blink!

With every turn, the strawberries spun,
Crafting a whirl that just looked like fun,
Their laughter echoed, a delight in the night,
In this lush retreat, everything felt right!

Nurtured Notions

In the garden of dreamy delights,
Tomatoes giggled through sunny sights,
Lettuce whispered "What's wrong with the peas?"
As cucumbers swayed with summer breezes.

The melons plotted a splashy race,
While mint gave a grin, and joined the chase,
Corn waved its tassels, feeling so proud,
While berries burst forth, singing out loud.

A mischievous grape had a spark of fun,
Said, "Let's play hide and seek, everyone!"
Oranges rolled, trying hard to hide,
While lemons just zested, laughing wide-eyed.

In the night, they basked under star's gaze,
Swapping tales in wonderful ways,
With every seed, a story flows,
In the nurture of laughter, the garden grows!

A Tasting of Time

In the orchard, giggles abound,
As apples drop without a sound.
A pear just sneezed, oh what a sight,
The oranges laugh, with all their might.

Berries bounce on berry stilts,
Claiming they're the kings of tilts.
Bananas slip in a comical race,
While cherries swing, keeping the pace.

Plum puns fly, juicy and bold,
Each line a tale that's never old.
With every taste, a chuckle is shared,
In this fruity world, no one is scared.

So gather 'round, let laughter ring,
For nature's humor is quite the thing.
With every bite, let giggles pop,
In this orchard where tickles don't stop.

The Aroma of Ripeness

Smells like mischief in the air,
Peaches blush with flair and care.
A lemon's twist makes no sense here,
While grapefruits giggle, what a cheer!

Plums in pajamas declare it's a binge,
While kiwis wear their fuzzy fringe.
Bananas peel, then slide away,
While tangerines dance, it's quite the ballet.

Melons joke about their size,
And laughter mixes with summer skies.
Pineapples crown their fruity heads,
As they make up stories in fruity beds.

So take a whiff, and laugh along,
With each aroma, you can't go wrong.
In this moment, joy will bloom,
As we feast on laughter, banishing gloom.

Whispers of the Grove

In the grove where laughter grows,
Tropical breezes hum with prose.
A coconut's tumble makes heads whirl,
While grapes tease each other, ready to twirl.

Mangoes lay back with a smug old grin,
While guavas gossip, spinning their spin.
Limes throw zingers, a citrus stand-up,
As jackfruit struts like it's won the cup.

Fig leaves rustle, sharing secrets loud,
While pomegranates boast, feeling proud.
Oranges joke with their zesty flair,
As they tumble 'round, without a care.

So join the fun in this lively scene,
Where every bite feels like a dream.
In this grove where hilarity thrives,
Let's taste the laughter that always survives.

Mellow Moments

Under the sun, the sweetness blooms,
Melons whisper in cool afternoon rooms.
Kiwis giggle behind their green mask,
While fruit flies dance, a silly task.

Fuzzy peaches lounge with ease,
Proclaiming, "Life's a breeze!"
Raspberries roll in fits of mirth,
As strawberries debate their worth.

Papayas share their dreamlike tales,
While figs burst out with fruity gales.
Cherries in hats parade with flair,
Spreading smiles, floating in the air.

So sink into this mellow scene,
Where laughter's ripe, and joy's routine.
In every slice, a chuckle waits,
Embracing the hilarity on our plates.

The Great Gathering

In a bowl on the table, they all convene,
The clumsy banana, the picky marine.
Grapes gossip softly, they laugh and they sway,
While apples just roll, in a comical way.

The orange gets jealous, of lemon's big grin,
When berries team up, oh, the noise they begin!
Kiwi brings tales, though few understand,
Causing all of them to just burst into planned.

Pineapple struts in with a crown on his head,
Declaring his party will go on instead.
But as all join in, the laughter unfolds,
As fruit salad danger is terribly told.

With everyone munching, and juggling their peels,
Some grapes get squished, it's a comedy of feels.
In the end, they're all happy, with friendships so bright,
The great fruit gathering, a delightful sight!

Nature's Sweet Caress

In the orchard, things twinkle with sunlight's embrace,
With cherries all giggling, and plums in a race.
The pears hang around, feeling quite out of place,
While peaches just blush, wearing nature's sweet grace.

A crunching of leaves signals apples nearby,
Who toss out some seeds, with a wink and a sigh.
The coconuts chuckle on high swaying trees,
As pomegranates joke, 'We're bursting with ease!'

The berries join forces, a colorful crew,
Singing about smoothies, oh, the fun they can brew!
But blueberries tumble, a clumsy ballet,
'Don't worry,' they say, 'We'll still be okay!'

In this dance of the harvest, humor takes flight,
Each bite brings a giggle, pure joy and delight.
Nature's sweet moments, with laughter, we'll share,
As we savor the bounty that hangs in the air.

Garden of Abundance

In the garden of joy, colorful gems grow,
Tomatoes in tutus, putting on a show.
Cucumbers prance with a gloriously green,
While carrots wear glasses, quite nerdy, unseen.

Zucchini's a bit bashful, hides under the leaves,
But when he gets brave, oh how the garden heaves!
Pumpkin jokes loudly, 'I'm here for the pie!'
While radishes giggle, just passing on by.

The lettuce starts dancing, it's quite the cut-up,
As beets roll their eyes, 'Are we in a hiccup?'
And onions all chuckle, they peel back the layers,
While peppers debate what spiciness wears.

At dusk, when the laughter has filled up the air,
And all have shared stories, each sprout takes a chair.
In this garden of humor, abundance is clear,
We feast on the giggles, with friends ever near!

Ripe with Promise

In the orchard, apples grin,
Telling tales of juicy sin.
Pears do jiggle, quite the sight,
Winking sweetly, oh what delight!

Cherries bounce, they love to tease,
Raspberries hang like small red keys.
Peaches chuckle, soft and round,
Ready for the bowl they found.

Plums wear hats of purple shame,
While bananas yell their name!
Lets have a party, come and see,
Let's celebrate with glee and glee!

But beware of the prune, beware indeed,
Shrinking smiles, a darkened deed.
In this harvest, oh what fun,
Watch them dance until they're done!

Fragrant Fables

Lemons laughing on the tree,
Slipping jokes so zestfully.
Oranges roll, they have no care,
Squeeze me more, they shout with flair!

Grapes are gossiping, oh so loud,
'We're the favorites,' they say proud.
But kiwis giggle, fuzzy boots,
'We've got style!' They hoot in suits.

Berries bouncing, quick on toes,
Everywhere their sweetness flows.
Dancing under sun's warm favor,
Juicy tales their friends will savor.

As their scents fill up the air,
Who could resist this fruity affair?
In this garden of mirthful crops,
Laughter echoes, never stops!

The Gathering Moon

Beneath the moon, berries glow,
Winks and giggles, don't you know?
Watermelons tell a tale,
Of sunset picnics, none can pale.

Pineapples plot with spiky crowns,
While cherries wear their shiny gowns.
Here comes the night, with laughter's hue,
A dance of sweetness, just for you.

Figs get flirty, on the sly,
While lychees bubble, oh my, oh my!
Nature's banquet, all aligned,
Under the moon, so sweetly twined.

Let's toast to jelly, jam and juice,
In this gathering, there's no excuse!
With every bite, the laughter croons,
While we bask 'neath the gathering moons!

Nature's Candy

In the garden, treats abound,
Sticky fingers all around.
Squash says, 'I'm not quite a sweet!'
'But I can make a really good treat!'

Tomatoes blush, so ripe and red,
They're guilty of the tales they've bred.
Cucumbers cool, playing it grand,
'In salads, we'll make our stand!'

Zucchini zips with a whispered cheer,
'Cooked or raw, I have no fear!'
Radishes ready, crisp with glee,
Nature's candy, can't you see?

Let's munch and crunch, let's share a laugh,
In this patch, we'll take a path.
A funny feast, so bright and dandy,
Let's cheer for nature's sweet candy!

Orchard Dreams

In an orchard bright and fair,
Apples giggle in the air.
They roll and bounce with such delight,
Making mornings feel just right.

Pears sit grinning, well aware,
Of the jokes they love to share.
Peaches blush, their laughter flows,
While cherries tell knock-knock shows.

The squirrels join the fruity talk,
Dancing round the grassy block.
With each bite, the laughter grows,
Who knew fruits could steal the show?

So next time you take a bite,
Remember how they felt that night.
In a world of zesty schemes,
Just dive into your orchard dreams!

Cascading Nectar

In a garden with a twist,
Honey drips, oh what a mist!
Bees in costumes, buzzing loud,
In their nectar, all are proud.

Mango swings from leafy bow,
With a giggle, 'Come and chow!'
Bananas slip, they make a slip,
On the juice, they take a trip.

Grapes hang tight, they form a gang,
'Watch out for the juice that tang!'
While pineapples wear tiny hats,
Riding waves on friendly chats.

As the colors splash and swirl,
Join the fun, just give a twirl!
With each taste, joy does unfold,
In their world of tales retold.

Colors of the Land

In a bowl of colors bright,
Fruits wear coats that are a sight.
Oranges laugh in sunny yellows,
While blues in berries dance like fellows.

Strawberries don their party hats,
Waltzing round with sneaky chats.
Lemons roll in citrus cheer,
Sour faces, but never fear!

Tropical vibes from coconuts,
They sway and shimmy, strut their guts.
While melons hum a juicy tune,
Underneath the lazy moon.

Colors mix with every bite,
Taste the joy, oh what a sight!
In a land where laughter flows,
Each crunchy bite, goodness shows.

The Tapestry of Taste

In a patchwork quilt of zest,
Every piece is truly blessed.
Kiwis bounce with vibrant flair,
Laughing at the pair they wear.

Raspberries spin in tiny round,
While they dance upon the ground.
An avocado takes a pose,
'The smoothest one, as everyone knows!'

Citrus friends join in the fun,
Playing tag until they run.
Pomegranate pops, a cheerful sight,
Juices splatter with delight!

So gather round, let laughter reign,
In the flavors, joy is plain.
In this tapestry we taste,
Moments shared are never waste.

Enchanted Harvest

Beneath the tree, I trip and fall,
A bouncing berry starts to call.
It rolls away, oh what a tease,
I chase it down with graceless ease.

The apples giggle in the breeze,
While lemon drops aim for my knees.
A fruit parade, oh what a sight,
I dance with joy, then lose my bite.

The nuts are laughing, it's no dream,
They tumble down in quite a scheme.
With every crunch, the laughter rings,
Who knew a harvest could have wings?

But here I stand, all sticky sweet,
With hands like glue and tangled feet.
The orchard's chaos, my delight,
A wacky world, oh what a sight!

Juicy Journeys

I set my sights on golden pears,
But then they sprout their naughty airs.
They dodge my grip, they leap and roll,
A slippery quest to catch my goal.

The grapes all giggle, stuck in vines,
They whisper secrets that are fines.
I trip on melons, land with a thud,
My juice-filled dreams now turn to mud.

A watermelon takes a stand,
It shouts, 'You'll never win this land!'
I laugh so hard, I almost weep,
A fruit-filled world, so fun and cheap!

At last I spy a peach so round,
I make my move, but hit the ground.
With every bite, I grin and cheer,
What a journey, full of cheer!

Petals and Pips

A blossom blooms—it starts to snicker,
A pumpkin laughs, 'Come on, be quicker!'
Flower petals dancing around,
While pips are popping on the ground.

Bananas swinging from the trees,
Crack a joke, they aim to please.
But when I slip, they all just stare,
As I fall flat, my fruit-to-air.

The cherries whistle, all in tune,
They float above like bright balloons.
Each little berry winks at me,
A fruity world, so wild and free!

But when I find a rogue grape vine,
The tangy thrill is just divine.
With giggles shared across the way,
Petals, pips—what a grand display!

Sweet Serenity

I lounge beneath the mango tree,
While all the fruits play hide and seek.
A coconut's too big to hide,
'I'm here!' it laughs, with lots of pride.

Peaches chatter, sharing glee,
Squeezing lemons, oh so free.
With every splash of juicy fun,
I giggle on, I'm not yet done!

A berry bus rolls down the lane,
'Takin' a trip, to sunny rain!'
I hop aboard, no time to lose,
With fruit as friends, I choose to cruise.

The laughter echoes, sweet and bright,
A harvest day, from morn till night.
So raise a glass, let's make a toast,
For fruity fun, we love the most!

The Orchard's Breath

In the orchard, apples laugh,
Pears wear hats and dance on grass.
Cherries giggle, bouncing round,
While plums play tag without a sound.

Peaches blush, they think they're stars,
Quirky grapes dreaming of fast cars.
Bananas slip, it's quite a sight,
As berries join in, taking flight.

Ciders bubbling in the breeze,
Snap! Goes a twig beneath the trees.
Silly squirrels have quite the spree,
Stealing snacks while singing glee.

So raise a toast to nature's jest,
A comical harvest, truly blessed!
In every bite, a chuckling cheer,
The orchard's breath brings joy so near.

Vintage of the Vine

Grapes in jackets, looking fine,
Whisper secrets of the vine.
Each drop of juice a funny tale,
Of drunken bees that tipped the pail.

Sipping wine with a twist of zest,
Sour lemons say, "We're the best!"
Oranges chuckle, plump and round,
As all the citrus spin around.

Ripe figs giggle in one big crew,
Joking about what's ripe and blue.
While berries play cards under the sun,
"A slice of pie? Oh, this is fun!"

Vintage vines with smiles so wide,
Bring joy and laughter, side by side.
Raise the glass, let laughter chime,
In this sweet vintage, all's sublime.

Syrupy Sunsets

Golden syrup drips from skies,
Laughing clouds with funny ties.
Sticky fingers, oh what a mess,
As pancakes dream of breakfast dress.

Maple trees wink with their charms,
While breakfast spreads out their arms.
Syrupy laughter, sweet delight,
Waffles prance into the night.

Butterflies flutter, spreading cheer,
As syrup whispers, "I am here!"
Toasting to the sticky sway,
Of creatures dancing in the fray.

Syrupy sunsets on the rise,
Bringing sweetness, what a surprise.
In every drop, a giggle lies,
With nature's humor under skies.

Orchard Serenade

Listen close to the singing trees,
Where laughter blends with buzzing bees.
Branches sway in silly rhymes,
As fruits compete for limelight times.

Coconuts cracking jokes so loud,
Making all their neighbors proud.
Watermelons, dressed in green,
Wobble and giggle, quite the scene.

Lemons roll like jesters on the ground,
While apples harmonize with sound.
A serenade of fruity fun,
In orchards where wild antics run.

So let the laughter fill the air,
In every corner, everywhere.
An orchard's song of joy we sing,
With every bite, let humor spring.

Nectarous Journeys

In a land where bananas yell,
And apples have stories to tell,
Grapes in their silky, purple dome,
Dream of the day they'll find a home.

Plums do a dance, twirl in the sun,
While cherries debate who's the most fun,
Pineapples joke, their leaves held high,
Saying, 'We're spiky, but give us a try!'

Oranges giggle, roll on the ground,
While peaches sing tunes that are sweet and profound,
Raspberries chuckle, 'We're just so cute,'
Their nectar, they say, tastes better with loot.

In this world of whimsy, so bright and bold,
Every bite has a story, every taste is gold.
With laughter and joy, they leap and fly,
A fruity adventure, oh me, oh my!

Vine and Verse

On the vine where the tomatoes lurk,
They plot and they plan, they're full of work.
A squash rolls by with a sly little grin,
'Why not join us? Where do I begin?'

Cucumbers cool with a cucumber air,
While carrots debate if they should wear flair.
Zucchini sticks out, 'I'm the chosen one!'
Potatoes just roll, having too much fun!

Berries chatter over their nectarous snack,
'We're not just sweet, we're flabbergasted, back!
Come join our party, under the sun,
With flavor and laughter, let's have some fun!'

So here's to the vines that twist and twirl,
Each veggie a tale in this whimsical whirl.
With laughter that dances through garden and field,
Their laughter and joy are the greatest yield!

Autumn's Orchard

The pumpkins plot with a gleam in their eye,
'This time of year, we never say die!'
They roll down the hill with a giggle and cheer,
'Wanna carve us up? Just don't bring a spear!'

Apples are boisterous, red like a blush,
Competing in races, they gleefully rush.
Cider is bubbling, the barrels rejoice,
'Let's have a party! Who's got the loud voice?'

Pears sway on branches, in soft autumn breeze,
Whispering secrets and cracking up trees.
While the nuts throw their shells in a playful huddle,
As squirrels scamper, creating a muddle.

With laughter descending like leaves on the ground,
These fruity shenanigans bubble around.
In the orchard of giggles, we gather and cheer,
'Let's toast to the harvest—now pour us a beer!'

Harvest Moon Melodies

Under the moon, the pears start to sway,
Singing and dancing, they're having a play.
Kiwi joins in with a zesty little spin,
Saying, 'I'm proud of my fuzzy green skin!'

Blackberries croon under stars, in a trance,
They tickle the night with their berry-like dance.
Ripe figs laugh loudly, their sweetness so bold,
'Who needs a crown when you feel this whole?'

Watermelons giggle, splitting with glee,
'Life is juicy, come slice it with me!'
While oranges chant from their sun-kissed tree,
'What's life without laughter? Just let it be!'

So gather around, as the melodies flow,
In the moonlight's embrace, let your laughter grow.
The harvest tonight is more than just food,
It's a fruity fiesta, a sweet, funny mood!

Nature's Offerings

The apples are grinning, red and round,
Dancing in baskets, all piled on the ground.
They whisper sweet secrets all day and night,
In the orchard's grand fancy, a comical sight.

The pears shake in laughter, a jig they perform,
Wobbling on branches, they're breaking the norm.
"What's a tree's favorite joke?" one claims with a cheer,
"Bark! Bark!" it chuckles, as leaves start to leer.

The strawberries wear spots, like polka-dot suits,
Playing hide and seek with their green leafy roots.
"Catch me if you can!" they taunt in delight,
While birds watch in wonder, what a fruity fight!

With cherries all giggling, they dangle so bright,
Swinging from twigs like they're ready for flight.
"Life's a bowl of cherries!" they sing in a glee,
In this merry grove, there's always room for me!

Essence of the Earth

Watermelons waddle, big and so round,
Rolling off picnic plates, they soar to the ground.
"I'm not just for summer!" a slice said with flair,
"Add salt for some giggles, if you dare!"

Lemons squint sunny, with zesty delight,
Slicing through puns like a warm sunny light.
"Why don't we play hide and seek?" one sour said,
"Because the lime's always up to no good ahead!"

Peaches parade in soft velvety skins,
On the kitchen counter, their mischief begins.
"Who's the juiciest?" they bet with a grin,
"Let's hold a contest and see who can win!"

Plums prance in purple, it's quite the charade,
Challenging teammates to a fruity parade.
"Snap a quick selfie!" they shout with delight,
Bursting with laughter in the warm evening light!

Blossoms and Berries

Raspberries chuckle in thickets so dense,
Daring brave squirrels to hop over the fence.
"Who's bold enough to munch us at noon?"
They boast and they giggle, "We make quite the tune!"

Blueberries shyly peek from a bush,
"I'm bluer than your mood!" they blush with a hush.
Wobbling on branches as if on a spree,
"Make room for the smoothies, it's just you and me!"

Blackberries bicker, in juicy debate,
"Are we more tart, or is that just fate?"
They wear tiny crowns, with thorns for a style,
In the berry world, there's always a trial!

Gooseberries giggle, a tangy delight,
Swinging in laughter as they bask in the light.
"Join us for giggles beneath every tree!"
In this jolly patch, they're always so free!

Sunlit Orchard Tales

Oranges grin widely, like suns in a rush,
"Life's a zest party!" they yell with a hush.
"Peel back the layers, see what you find,
A citrusy giggle that's one of a kind!"

Mangoes are flipping, with moves so unique,
Whirling in bowls for the taste buds to sneak.
"Who needs ice cream?" says one with a flair,
"When you're fresh and juicy, nothing else can compare!"

Coconuts clink, like a tropical band,
"Join us for laughs, we'll all take a stand!"
With shells that are tough, but hearts soft as fluff,
They shake to the rhythm, chanting, "That's enough!"

Grapes gather round, like a giddy old crew,
"Let's stomp till we drop, with laughter so true!"
In this sunlit orchard, with laughter galore,
Fruity adventures are always in store!

Cider and Sunshine

Under trees, we gather round,
With jugs of joy and laughter's sound.
A splash and slosh, our hearts aglow,
In liquid sun, our giggles flow.

Apples dance, they twist and twirl,
In bubbling cauldrons, they swirl and swirl.
We sip and snicker, our cheeks go red,
As sweet drops fall from happy heads.

Bubbles rise, a fizzy cheer,
Each gulp boasts, I'm glad you're here.
The sunbeams tickle, the breeze delivers,
As we toast to life with cider quivers.

So raise your glass, let worries cease,
In this orchard, we find our peace.
With laughter's voice, we sing along,
In cider's warmth, we all belong.

Petals to Plate

We prance with flowers on our plates,
A feast of color, oh, what great mates!
Daisy sandwiches, tulip stew,
Gourmet giggles for me and you.

Violets sprinkle on our cakes,
Each bite taken, our chuckle shakes.
With honey drips and laughter's tease,
We munch our blooms with utmost ease.

Handfuls of petals, a salad fresh,
Whimsical wonders from nature's mesh.
We share a bite, then burst in glee,
Trading flavors of jubilee.

At lunch today, it's pure delight,
With every chew, we take to flight.
In petal bliss, let's celebrate,
With every laugh, our friends await.

The Flavorful Turn

Round and round in the kitchen we race,
Chopping, mixing, a tasty embrace.
Peppers giggle as onions cry,
In a pan of play, our spirits fly.

Tomatoes swing in salsa steps,
While garlic whispers its secret reps.
Zucchini jokes, they grow quite bold,
Each chop a story waiting to unfold.

We stir and taste, oh, what is this?
A symphony of flavors we can't quite miss.
With every scoop, our spoons collide,
In this flavorful turn, we take wild strides.

So let's sauté our cares away,
In this banquet of joy, we laugh and sway.
Each bite a chuckle, a savory round,
In this kitchen dance, pure bliss is found.

A Symphony of Sap

In the forest, trees burst with glee,
Their sweet elixirs flow wild and free.
The sap drips down like a ticklish tease,
Collecting smiles from giggling trees.

Maple melodies in the springtime air,
With syrupy songs, we sway with flair.
A splash on pancakes makes us cheer,
In gooey delight, we shed a tear.

Old trunks whisper, 'Join the fun!'
With sticky fingers, our work's not done.
We laugh and lick, our bellies round,
In this syrup swirl, joy's always found.

So raise a toast with a sugary grin,
In nature's orchestra, let's all join in.
With every drip, our hearts will clap,
In this sweet affair, we'll revel in sap.

Juicy Revelations

In the grove where laughter sways,
Oranges giggle in bright arrays.
They roll around on summer grass,
Chasing bees—their bumpy mass.

Lemons zap with zesty jokes,
Telling tales to laughing blokes.
A pear tripped, did a little dance,
Said, "Take me home, give me a chance!"

Berries burst with sticky glee,
Shouting out 'dance with me, me, me!'
They splatter juice, a colorful sight,
Painting shoes with their delight!

Bananas slip, oh what a sight,
Banana peels causing sheer fright.
But everyone laughs, no one's mad,
Silly antics make us glad!

Seasonal Serenade

Cherries laugh from their tall trees,
Swinging lightly in the breeze.
They gossip sweetly, red and bold,
Whispering secrets of stories untold.

Apples parade in cardinal hues,
Joking about their farmer's shoes.
'Wear your boots, it's muddy here!'
They giggle while spinning round with cheer.

Peaches blush in the summer sun,
Sassy shake, oh what fun!
They play hide-and-seek all day,
Rolling off in a playful way.

Grapes play catch with a jolly cheer,
Happily bouncing here and there.
They squish and pop with every throw,
Leaving juice trails all aglow!

Garden's Palette

In the garden, colors clash,
Tomatoes wink, they're quite brash.
Carrots laugh with bright orange zest,
Claiming they're surely the best dressed.

Radishes prank in stripes of red,
Telling tales by the garden bed.
They boast of crunch, the crunchiest cheer,
While peas dance and jump in fear.

Zucchini jokes in their green coats,
Saying, 'Look, I can float on boats!'
Squash giggles as it twists in line,
Scribbling rhymes like a poet divine.

Broccoli rumbles with hearty laughs,
Sharing stories about silly gaffes.
It's all a jolly, colorful mess,
Nature's fun—yes, nothing less!

Sunkissed Offerings

Watermelons sing in the sun,
Happily splashing, just for fun.
Seeds dance like little stars,
Spitting games—it's who the best is by far!

Pineapples wear crowns, so proud,
Joking they're the funkiest in the crowd.
They dance to rhythms tropical and sweet,
Twisting to their own fruity beat.

Coconuts crack with a hearty cheer,
Sharing tales of the ocean near.
They chuckle and bounce to the beat,
Making the whole party complete!

Papayas giggle with a twist,
Saying 'Don't take life too serious, just gist!'
Each bite a laugh, a happy tease,
In this warm sun, we find our ease.

Blossoms and Bounty

In the garden, squirrels make a fuss,
Chasing each other just to discuss.
I spy a tomato, plump and round,
With a thrill, it rolls, where's it found?

Bees dance about, sipping their drink,
While I stare and just start to think.
Should I chase them off with a hat?
Or just join in on their little chat?

Lemonade lemons, hiding in green,
Trying to act like they're all unseen.
But one little fruit had quite the sass,
Said, "I'm the one making everyone's glass!"

An apple fell right on my toe,
It laughed and rolled, saying, 'Take it slow.'
I waved goodbye, it winked real sly,
Who knew my snack could say goodbye?

Nature's Confection

A cherry tree wore a sour frown,
The crow nearby was too round.
Pointing at berries, ripe and sweet,
Cherries yelled, 'We can take the heat!'

Peaches in robes of fuzzy pride,
Taunt the apricots who hide.
'We've got juice, what do you lack?'
While plums just strut, giving no crack!

A banana slipped – oh what a sight!
It juggled its way into the night.
Lemons laughed, bright as a sun,
Said, 'Let's roll, and join in the fun!'

Grapes whispered secrets from the vine,
While snackers debated, 'Who's more divine?'
Berries giggled, short and stout,
'Sharing giggles, that's what it's about!'

Savoring Sunlight

Pineapples wearing crowns so tall,
Scale the heights but somehow fall.
They land on coconuts, what a splash!
Sipping sunshine — they make quite a smash!

Oranges argue in zesty glee,
'Who's the juiciest? Oh, that's me!'
But lemons chime in, tart and bright,
'We're the zingers that feel just right!'

A wild kiwi took to the stage,
Dancing with flair like an animal caged.
'Take it easy!' yelled the melon troupe,
As chortling berries joined the loop!

Sunflowers joined in this fruity dance,
Waving bright petals – oh what a chance!
To taste the fun, in flavors burst,
With nature's laughter, we all are immersed!

The Colors of Abundance

Red strawberries sport feathery hats,
While green limes squabble, like pesky rats.
'We're the star!' the raspberries shout,
As blueberries nibble on what's about!

Mangoes lounge, their golden glow,
Under the shade, hearing the show.
'The juiciness wins,' they all declare,
As pineapples cheer from way over there!

Plums flip-flop in shades so bright,
Arguing over who's the delight.
'Just burn the pie, it's quite the sin,'
Said the peaches, 'But we'll still win!'

A tangerine rolled, laughing aloud,
As oranges settled, feeling so proud.
Together they sang 'The Juicy Crew,'
In a combo of flavors, all fresh and new!

Nature's Abundant Tapestry

In the garden, colors clash,
A purple pear met a yellow flash.
They argued loudly, much to our glee,
'I'm more delicious!' said the apple tree.

The berries giggled in a juicy bunch,
While oranges plotted a lunchtime crunch.
Bananas slipped and fell with a yell,
'You'll never pick me, I'm under this shell!'

But here in the sunlight, all is fair,
Especially when melons start to share.
A watermelon rolled with a great big grin,
'Join the fun, everyone, let the feast begin!'

So grab a basket, let laughter ring,
Among these edibles, joy's in the fling.
With nature's chaos, we slice and chew,
In this wild party, there's room for you!

Earth's Edible Treasures

A pineapple wore a crown of green,
Swearing that it's the best we've seen.
But lemons chimed, 'We're tart but bright!'
'At least we know how to start a fight!'

The grapes were hanging just out of sight,
Whispering secrets of a fruitful night.
'Let's tell the world of our sweet romance,'
As cherries danced in a haphazard prance.

Olive branches waved with cheeky flair,
'Our oil is golden, beyond compare!'
'But basil scoffed, 'You're swimming in brine!'
As mint danced in, all fresh and divine.

So take a sweet tour down this silly lane,
With mixtures and flavors, we'll never be plain.
For in this orchard of laughter and fun,
Our edible treasures have only begun!

Harvested Whispers

The pumpkins giggled, round and stout,
'We're the kings of the harvest, there's never a doubt!'
But carrots below shot back with a root,
'In the soil, my friend, we'll outgrow your fruit!'

Peaches, with blush, were quick to agree,
'You'll never outshine our sweet jubilee!'
Yet tomatoes blushed red, feeling quite bold,
'Ketchup on fries—now that never gets old!'

Now berries were chuckling, all plump and round,
'We've got the jams that make hearts pound!'
But grapefruits exclaimed, 'We're bitter, we'll fight!'
'Just sprinkle some sugar and we're feeling right!'

As the laughter swells, oh what a show,
From veggies to sweets, let the good times flow.
In this silly harvest, joy is the goal,
Let's toast with some cider, come on, let's roll!

In the Orchard's Embrace

In the orchard, apples take a seat,
Telling tall tales of their juicy feat.
'I've seen the world from a tree so high,
Just last week, I almost touched the sky!'

The oranges bounced in a jolly parade,
'Who needs a plane? We're citrus made!'
But bananas chimed in, feeling so spry,
'Why don't we peel our fears and fly?'

Cherries were giggling, their stems in a knot,
'We're small, but together we've got quite a plot!'
While the grapes agreed, stitched in a vine,
'We'll throw a party—sip sweet nectar divine!'

So join the fun, taste this fruit-filled spree,
With laughter and chuckles, so wild and free.
In nature's embrace, where silliness sways,
Let's dance through the orchards, brightening our days!

Picnic by the Orchard

We packed a bag with snacks so sweet,
And headed to where the branches meet.
A squirrel stole our sandwich on a dare,
We laughed so hard, he was quite the flair.

The apples rolled while the bees took flight,
Chasing our laughter from morning to night.
A watermelon split, oh what a scene,
We squealed like kids, feeling just like teens.

Lemons squirted while we danced around,
Orange peels slipped; we toppled to the ground.
Between the giggles, we spotted a bear,
He waved us goodbye, as if he did care.

As shadows grew long, and sun dipped low,
We packed up our laughter, rode off in a row.
With crumpled napkins, we smiled so wide,
A picnic with happiness, never to hide.

Tangy Tidings

I bit into a lime, what a nasty surprise,
Puckered up my face, made me roll my eyes.
A grape dared to bounce, wanting freedom's flare,
"Catch me if you can!" it laughed in mid-air.

The kiwi yelled, "I'm fuzzy but nice!"
While berries debated who'd be the next slice.
Citrus then chimed in, "Let's mix it up!"
A fruit salad party? Oh, fill up my cup!

Bananas slipped by, acting all cool,
While peaches just lounged, breaking all the rules.
We laughed as they giggled, all shades of bright,
A tangy reunion, what a silly sight!

At the end of the day, with juice on our chin,
We formed a parade and danced in a spin.
With flavors in tow, and a grin ear to ear,
In our fruity kingdom, we'll always cheer!

Echoes of Bounty

An orchard's a concert; the pears like to sing,
Jamming with cherries in a fruity fling.
'Watch me!" said peach, with a twirl and a twist,
While nuts rolled their eyes, they didn't want to miss.

Grapefruits grumbled, feeling quite sour,
But giggled soon after, gaining sweet power.
The vines had a story; the figs knew it well,
Of a heist by the apples, oh what a tale to tell!

In this fruity fiesta, everyone danced,
Papayas and plums briefly glanced.
Mango declared, with a wink and a throw,
'If you blend us together, you really should know!'

As twilight approached, they formed a parade,
Celebrating their quirks in a delectable shade.
With echoes of laughter, the orchard did sway,
A bounty of silliness, come join the play!

Charm of the Orchard

In the orchard's embrace, where laughter prevails,
We'd jest with the peaches, swap tall fruity tales.
Bubbles of cider danced in the breeze,
While oranges and limes played tag with the leaves.

'The sun can't catch me!" crowed a bold berry,
While cherries giggled, feeling quite merry.
A fig wore a crown, declaring it a fest,
While nuts tried to judge who looked the best!

With each juicy moment, we spun with delight,
As apples threw seeds, aiming for flight.
Lemonade chuckled, sweet and so tangy,
Inviting us all to get a bit fancy.

We wrapped up our fun as the day settled down,
With puns and some juice, we turned it around.
The charm of the orchard danced in our hearts,
A fruity adventure where silliness starts.

Juicy Secrets of Autumn

Red apples grinning, they can't keep still,
Dancing in baskets, what a fun thrill!
Pumpkins with faces, oh what a sight,
Hiding behind fences, giving a fright.

Crisp leaves a-crunching beneath our feet,
Squirrels are hoarding, oh what a treat!
Acorns are falling, it's a nutty race,
Let's find a treasure, in this funny place.

Cider that's bubbling, spiced just right,
Tickling our noses, a warm delight!
Caramel jackets on apples so sweet,
What a concoction, who can compete?

Autumn's a stand-up, a true comic show,
With nature's own antics, stealing the show!
So let's all laugh as we gather 'round,
For juicy secrets just waiting to be found.

Bounty of the Grove

In the grove, oh what a feast,
Where berries giggle and sweetness increased!
Cherries on branches, laughing in red,
Taking a nap in their leafy bed.

Bananas are slipping, oh what a fall,
Hilarious chaos, they bounce off the wall!
Oranges roll by with a citrus-y grin,
You'd think they were playing a wild game of spin.

Peaches are fuzzy, they tickle your palm,
Whispering secrets, so sweet and calm!
Pears make us ponder, with thoughts like these:
What if they giggled, or danced in the breeze?

Come one, come all, for the humorous stash,
Where every bite leads to a belly-laugh bash!
In the grove, we gather, all smiles on display,
For nature's own comedy, exciting and gay!

Sunkissed Abundance

Sunshine's a trickster, warming the day,
While berries in sunlight are chasing the play!
Grapes in a cluster, they chatter and cheer,
Hoping for parties, their moment is near.

Mangoes are winking, they know they are grand,
Doing the tango, they dance in the sand!
Pineapples wearing their crowns without shame,
Who knew that these guys could play the game?

Coconuts giggle as they roll in a line,
Sipping on breezes, feeling so fine.
Kiwi with glasses, oh what a sight,
Reading a book in the warm golden light.

Let's savor the laughter, the warmth and the cheer,
With nature's fun bounty, we gather right here!
In this sunkissed wonder, laughter captivates,
Creating memories that time celebrates.

The Sweetness of Twilight

In twilight's embrace, all colors collide,
Where berries are blushing, with secrets to hide.
Night brings a soft glow, fruit dreams in the air,
Hilarity lingers, with joy everywhere.

Figs dressed in purple, a dapper delight,
Telling the stories of day into night!
Lemons are giggling, all zesty and bright,
Their puns make us chuckle, what a pure sight!

Plums in their pajamas, so snug and so round,
Whisper soft jokes that could easily drown.
Limes spin in circles, so cheerful and spry,
Bouncing like bunnies as twilight slips by.

Gathered in shadows, we toast to the fun,
With baskets of sweetness, our laughter's begun!
In twilight's embrace, let the silliness flow,
For the sweetness of life always steals the show.

A Cornucopia of Color

In a basket bright, a debate ensues,
Are you red like a clown, or green like old shoes?
The oranges giggle, the bananas just roll,
While grapes are too busy playing the troll.

Lemons make faces, sour with glee,
Whispering secrets: "A pie? Not for me!"
Peaches toss tails, think they're so clever,
But who'll take the plunge? Not the apple, oh never!

Strawberries dance, with seeds on their suits,
Bouncing around like young, wild recruits.
"Let's host a party," the cherries all cry,
"Just don't let the kid with the knife wander by!"

In the end, what a colorful crew,
Making a mess and a splash, who knew?
Together they chuckle, in playful delight,
Who knew a vegetable could taste so right?

Whispering Vines

In the garden of giggles, the cucumbers plot,
"Are we vegetables, or just laughing a lot?"
The tomatoes are blushing, red cheeked in sun,
While the basil is teasing, just having some fun.

The pumpkins roll by, big grins on their face,
"Let's carve out some joy, leave a silly trace!"
But the squash is quite shy, hides under a leaf,
Mumbling softly, "This is beyond belief!"

The peppers are spicy, with jokes that they share,
Poking fun at the carrots, without a care.
"Orange is brave, but is it a fruit?"
While zucchini chimes in, "I'm neither, to boot!"

As laughter erupts, the vine starts to sway,
Who knew in the garden, we'd play all day?
With sunshine and giggles, and breezes so fine,
Who could resist this? It's a vine-y design!

The Plentiful Path

Down the road of harvest, they giggle and glide,
Where pumpkins have eyes and the corn comes with pride.
"Is that really a carrot, or just having a laugh?"
A broccoli whispers, "I'm family, not staff!"

On leafy green pathways, they twirl and they sway,
The tomatoes blush deeper as they see some sun play.
"Let's have a race!" shouts a sprightly taro,
But beats all the shapes, just a gnarled old potato.

Cucumbers roll over, laughing so loud,
While sprouts stand up tall, feeling super proud.
"Why can't we all dance?" a bell pepper sighs,
And the radishes cheer with their bright little eyes.

But alas, it's a twist on this bumpy old road,
They bump into squash, who's dropped their corn load.
In the end, they unite for a fruit salad feast,
Together they chuckle—what a peculiar beast!

Sundrenched Harvest

Under sun-kissed rays, the laughter does bloom,
Lettuce does jiggle in the warm garden room.
"Do you think we could footloose?" the kale starts to tease,
While chives wiggle sideways in the gentle breeze.

Tomatoes gossip, with seeds in their chat,
"Do I look a bit squishy, or just a bit fat?"
"Stop worrying, friend!" says a sweet little pea,
"Just embrace your juiciness, be happy and free!"

While those flashy pink berries roll round with a cheer,
They're dripping with sweetness, 'tis the best time of year!
"Come one and come all, let's gather and sing,
With sun on our backs, we can all be the king!"

As the baskets fill full, and the smiles abound,
Together they dance on this fertile ground.
So let's raise a toast in a most rambunctious way,
To all of the produce that brightens our day!

www.ingramcontent.com/pod-product-compliance
Lightning Source LLC
Chambersburg PA
CBHW062111280426
43661CB00086B/447